Ode to the Unknown

Where Good May Not Always Prevail

Lisa Hale Vandergriff

Waldenhouse Publishers
Elberfeld, IN

Ode to the Unknown: Where Good May Not Always Prevail

Published by Waldenhouse Publishers, LLC.
Elberfeld, Indiana
812-549-7536 www.waldenhouse.com
Printed in the U.S.A.
Cover Art by Elaine Foster
ISBNs:
978-1-970530-01-8 (paperback)
978-1-970530-02-5 (hardcover)
978-1-970530-03-2 (ebook)
Library of Congress Control Number: 2026909751
A reflective poetry collection exploring identity, expectation, love, and resilience. Structured around moments of transition, the poems trace a path toward self-acceptance and the enduring presence of hope.

Dedication

First and foremost, all glory goes to God for giving me the ability to paint with words.

Also, this is for my children—Morgan, Delana, Frank. They endured a somewhat wacky mother, and they did so with a joy and patience I will always admire. Each of them is uniquely different and beautiful.

In addition, a catalyst, by definition, is a substance that increases the rate of a chemical reaction without itself undergoing any permanent change. I can only speak for myself—and that is where we are.

This collection of poetry came about because someone became that catalyst, reigniting a passion I had buried deep within myself, forever tying our hearts. Sometimes, chance encounters are the most meaningful.

Finally, this is for myself and everyone else who has felt like they needed to hide or suppress their passion and emotions.

Thank you to my sister Elaine for allowing me to use her artwork for the cover.

Contents

Where It All Begins

Opening Doors

The Heart Matters Part One

The Heart Matters Part Two

The Heart Breaks

The Heart Shatters

Hope for a New Beginning

Making Sense of It All

Why It Matters

Special Poems for My Family and Friends

Where It All Begins

Alas, I May Starve

The empty cupboard was much to bear.
The unlit stove far too cold.
Hope and dreams of the future seemed,
Lost in the distance fold.

What once I thought I could live without,
Not food nor warmth nor love.
The tender touch of a maiden's hand,
Was desired not yet earned.

The wine was bitter, the stove was cold,
With nothing for my heart's desire.
I longed for the taste of sweet sweet wine,
And the warmth of the roaring fire.

More than that my hunger grew,
With pain unfelt before.
I cannot quench my thirst.
The desire burned to my core.

For fate had dealt an evil hand,
That time perhaps might solve.
Still I hungered more and more,
Hoping for some resolve.

Cruel is the hunger that leads to thirst,
With no relief in sight.
Alas, I may starve,
Giving in without a fight.

On a Rainy December Day

What can warm the heart and the soul
On rainy days like this?
The sound of the rain drops
Feel much like a tender kiss.

The rhythm much too steady
Not nearly quick enough,
To quench the desire of my fire
Giving into lust.

Perhaps the touch of your lips,
Gently brushing mine,
Might well be enough,
To fulfill my heart's desire.

For time is a funny thing.
It holds tight to our will.
Never letting go of us.
And never standing still.

We cannot have that moment lost.
The touch of our first embrace,
The first kiss upon my lips,
When your breath I taste.

Into your eyes I gaze.
Knowing all the risk.
All of me will belong to you,
After that first kiss.

I Wasn't Looking at the Clock

I wasn't looking at the clock.
But time did not stand still.
I was only thinking of the moment.
Wondering if it was real.

With a kiss and a gentle touch,
I hoped for my heart's desire.
But my love was pushed away,
Before starting the fire.

My body ached for his touch.
The smell of his tender kiss,
To taste the warmth of his breath,
Was more than I could risk.

I knew as he knew,
That if we were to meet,
I would belong to him,
Every ounce of me.

I was terrified of the thought.
I gave into my fear.
Here alone I sit.
Wishing he was here.

Not sure even if I could,
In a moment that will last,
Longing for his tender touch,
Would I change the past?

Though We May Never Meet

Time is what time is.
Never standing still.
It is what gauges our lives,
Future, now and then.
We cannot touch it.
It has no smell,
Or even a sweet taste.
Sometimes we value not.
Other times we waste.
Often wish it stopped.
Each passing moment,
Each breaking dawn,
Each shadow upon the ground,
Reminds us of special things,
Of love not yet found,
Despite our wishes,
Our heartfelt hope,
It is here to let us know.
Though paths may cross,
With purposeful intent.
A moment lost,
Is a moment we never see again.

If You Could See Through My Eyes

If you could see through my eyes,
I wonder how you would feel?
Would you still long for me?
Could we still be friends?

If you could feel what I feel,
Would it change your ways?
Would you tread more lightly?
Or simply walk away?

Does my passion scare you?
For it scares me too.
I am afraid to lose myself,
By giving myself to you.

You say I do not know what I want,
And that is not okay for you.
But you never asked me what it was,
So how can you know that's true?

But since you did not ask.
I will tell you now.
I want to love deeply,
Like I never have before.

So deeply that it hurts,
Not from a simple kiss,
I want to feel it all,
Your body, mind, and soul.

Kissing a Frog

The first kiss was a gentle brush,
Just enough to taste.
The second kiss was just enough,
To make my heart race.
The third kiss was long and deep,
With a passionate embrace.
The next kiss was just enough,
To take my breath away.
The last first kiss,
Our first embrace,
Our bodies intertwined,
Stirring the fire of desire,
Only quenched by time.

Not All of Me at Once

To share my thoughts was one thing,
The stuff stored in my mind.
The things that made me who I am,
Often funny at times,

To share my passion with another,
I hesitate at first.
The thought of such exposure,
With a chance of getting hurt,

To share my emotions what I feel,
Way deep down inside,
Brought with it a risk,
I had worked hard to hide.

To share my soul who I am,
The very essence of me,
Meant taking a chance,
Letting others in, letting them see.

To share a heart that easily breaks,
The beating of a life,
Shows some compassion,
While letting in the light.

To share all of me, every single ounce,
But not all of me at once,
My mind, my heart, my soul,
But let me trust in you first.

Intentions

I thought that his moving fast,
Was a sign he did not see.
He had no real interest,
In getting to know me.

Perhaps I might be right.
Perhaps I may be wrong.
Only he knows for sure,
What words are in his song.

Maybe it is just his way,
The wiring of his brain.
He may need the touch,
Much like kissing in the rain.

I fear I have judged his harshly.
Though that was not my intend.
I should have listened more closely,
And felt what he meant.

It takes a lot of trust,
To strip way the night.
To walk naked into darkness,
Hoping to find the light.

But when all worldly things are gone,
While leaving things to fate.
The vulnerability of that first moment,
May lead to something great.

Words

Do you think it is by coincidence,
The words that we choose?
Do we try to paint a picture?
Or with them confuse?

Do we bait our audience,
With figurative language cues?
Hoping they will draw conclusions,
From our many clues?

Every statement has two meanings,
Both literal and implied.
We lure our reader to conclude,
Which thought they will abide.

Some statements are more obvious,
Other not near as clean.
We give subtle hints,
Hoping only a few will see.

In the security of our words,
Our world we try to paint.
Afraid to share it out right,
Leaving much to fate.

What Stirs Your Heart to Tears?

What stirs your heart to tears?
Is it the intimacy of an embrace?
Is it the touch of a lover?
Is it the things left undone?
Or the one that got away?
Is it the brilliant kiss on a summer's day?
Or the moonlight dancing on the water's edge?
What makes your heart race?
What do you care for so deeply?
What is it that you cannot share?
Out of fear or other reasons?
What makes it safe to hide?
Hiding from others or hidden from yourself?
Both are meant to protect?
I shared my thoughts, my heart and fears.
I shared with you what brings me to tears.
I shared the hopes of a love unknown.
I ask you now, though I know
What stirs your heart to tears?

Silence

I feel it in the silence,
Words you will not speak.
Not because you do not want to,
But you feel it makes you weak.

I feel it in the silence,
The pain you have endured.
The loss and the love unspoken,
Even when you are sure.

I feel it in the silence,
The way you think it should be.
How you can distance yourself from love,
By not letting others see.

I feel it in your silence,
The fear is real for you.
You push others away.
You deny it, but it's true.

I feel it in your silence,
You have hope despite our start.
That love will find its way,
Into both of our hearts.

To Know You

I know nothing of your heart.
You have shared little with me,
Your thoughts and your feelings,
Only some of your beliefs.

I have only been guessing,
What is deep inside?
I feel there is much more.
You feel the need to hide.

For who you really are.
I try my best to see.
But you hold tight to this truth,
Which is difficult for me.

I want to know all of you.
To the very depth of your soul,
The good, the bad and the ugly,
The things you have not told.

I want you to trust me always,
Like no one you have before.
Knowing that you are safe with me.
I want this and so much more.

Opening Doors

Lost Love

Our hopes are often built,
In the depths of our mind,
Our reality skewed,
Diluted over time.

Sometimes it is hard to tell
What is real or fantasy.
Like the origin of the wind,
That calms the roughest seas.

The direction that the wind blows
Makes a difference to some.
Like the beat of a heart,
Looking for lost love.

Love lost or never found,
Is the biggest tragedy they say.
To searching aimlessly for years,
For the one that got away.

Would It Make a Difference?

When darkness comes
For our hearts,
And the cold wind blows
For our souls,
Where can hope be found?
Do we lose ourselves
In the darkest shadows,
Walk alone in the coldest night,
Where no one will find us?
What do we dare change
To help us find our way?
Is it found in tomorrow's dreams,
Or is it lost within today's reality?
If it is for tomorrow?
How long do we wait?
Do we wait with patience?
Do we hope endlessly?
Do we part ways with the dream,
Chasing another into the night?
Do we leave it all to fate,
Or is it in God's hands?
What would we change?
If we could change anything,
And would it make a difference?

What Rose Goes Untouched

What rose goes untouched,
Until the snow does fall?
Loses not her beauty,
Despite winter's call.

When the snow does fall,
Bringing an end to warmer days,
Should we dwell in our misery,
Or try to find our way?

Darkness always gives way to light,
Much as love rules over hate.
Hiding in the shadows,
Will not change our fate?

It is what it is.
Some things remain the same.
The past being one of them.
If we could, would we change?

Does it matter our heart's desire?
Moments sitting in the dark,
Wondering if light will find a way,
To open up our hearts?

Unresolved

I sent him what he asked.
I shared my heart and soul.
It was hard for me to let him in,
If the truth be told.

His silence speaks volumes,
Not of how he feels for me,
But of how he must treat others.
It is very clear to see.

He wanted things his way,
Or at least that is what he said.
But when I gave him what he wanted,
It was as if it were left dead.

I wonder if he knows what he wants.
I thought he made it clear.
Sometimes the journey is easy;
It's the destination that we fear.

I thought we had a connection,
At least an emotional bond.
Maybe I played my cards too soon,
Perhaps it was too strong.

Now I am the one confused.
Where do these waters lead?
Do I give up on him altogether,
Unsure of what he needs?

Myth of the Other Half

His silence spoke volumes.
Sometimes it is words unsaid.
That leads us to the greater knowledge,
Found within ourselves.

Wisdom is a trying concept.
One most of us could use.
Instead we stumble in the darkness,
Lost, hopeless, and confused.

I did not mean to like him.
But I feel it is so much more.
He may well be the other half,
That I have been searching for.

The Cave

We try to hide the truth we seek.
We think the truth makes us weak.
We protect ourselves as we walk alone,
Hoping that others will not know.

We hide ourselves within a cave,
Facing inward toward the shade.
Shadows dance, sing, and play;
In the darkness, we plan to stay.

Afraid to see what the light might bring,
We hide ourselves from everything.
Hope often gives in to fear;
Within the cave, nothing is clear.

We dare not turn to face the light.
The darkness protects us in the night.
The sun makes shadows dance,
We do not care to take a chance.

The entrance of the cave grows bright.
We choose to not face the light.
Some will die who could be saved,
Because they refuse to leave the cave.

When It's 4 AM

I woke thinking what it must be like,
To kiss him and be held tight,
To feel the warmth of his skin,
To be deeply in love with him,
To have his hands gently caress,
To have hope for all the rest,
To give in to my wildest desire,
Knowing only he can stir that fire.

At 4 AM, things are unclear.
There is darkness, cold, and fear.
As I lay awake at night,
I wish he was here to hold me tight.

But he is not here, not today.
So alone, I lay awake,
Wondering if the time will ever come,
When our hearts and bodies will be one.

Wine

The wine was sweet upon my lips.
A taste I longed to feel.
The fruit and passion of my desire
Were all my thoughts required.

The glass was delicate to my touch.
My fingers caressed the rim.
The coolness of the taste,
The sleekness of the stem.

As my lips kissed the glass,
Slowly tasting my desire,
One single sip of the poison
Would not quench my fire.

A second, even more sweet,
With a deeper, longer taste,
The fire burned inside of me,
A passion unwilling to face.

So, as the evening grew,
More wine I did desire.
My thirst could not be quenched,
Nor could my heart's fire.

Is There Power in the Truth?

I almost changed myself for him,
Despite what I know is true.
You can only pretend so much,
Before you must be you.

I cannot blame him; it is not his fault.
He did not ask me to change,
But the outcome, such that it is,
Still remains the same.

I promised myself long ago
I would not let this happen again,
But I was so drawn to him,
I wanted to be more than friends.

He wanted me, so he said.
A clear message was sent.
I could not change who I am;
That was my sole intent.

So I pushed him away and let him think
That he had decided not to meet.
I let him keep his ego intact,
But in my heart, I know the facts.

The Darkest Day

When a heart is closed to the light,
It staggers hopelessly in the night.
The sun cannot venture near;
All hope is lost and unclear.

The darkness that envelopes the soul
Leaves us lonely, weak, and cold.
We wander aimlessly into the night,
Fearful of the morning light.

But when morning waits too long,
We lose our faith, no longer strong.
When hope gives into lonely fear,
There is no one else to make things clear.

We continue to wander hopeless in the dark,
Afraid of the light within our heart.
But there is but one day, once a year,
When the night captures all our fear.

When daylight refuses to abide,
We search for hope deep inside.
Not always true to what we feel,
We wait patiently for hearts to heal.

In the darkness, lonely and cold,
Our deepest desires are what we hold.
Time may or may not make things clear;
Nothing good can come from fear.

For fear freezes us much like snow.
At some point, we must let go,
Walk the path we were meant to run,
Until we can clearly see the sun.

Darkness is but for a season.
In our heart, we know the reason.
But if we give into the darkest day,
Will we be able to walk away?

Opening the Door to My Heart

I let the darkness surround my soul.
There was no light, the true be told.
I woke each morning to my surprise,
Wondering where my future lies.

Each day I walked the same walk,
Met the same people, had the same talk.
I opened doors that would not close,
To unknown truths that must be told.

Mornings grew more weary still,
Nothing new, nothing real.
Hope had escaped, gone it seems;
I was left with only unfulfilled dreams.

Time was not standing still at all.
Somewhere deep down, I felt a call
To push away my darkest thoughts,
To live again, no matter the cost.

By chance, a stranger passing by
Could see beyond my deepest lies.
All my hopes and fears depart;
He opened the door to my heart.

Now I see as I saw before.
I was the one holding the door.
I had the power; it was always me.
He just came to set me free.

The Heart Matters

Part One

The Swim

The ocean kisses the shore each night.
The stars dance at twilight.
The moon, a stranger to no one,
Rarely seen by the rising sun.

The warm water against my skin
Makes me feel young again.
To glide endlessly through the waves
Is something I will always crave.

My body being caressed like this
Is like a kiss upon my lips,
Tightly intertwined as much,
Feeling like a lover's touch.

But with each breaking wave
It is like being buried in the grave.
To fight for air, to surface, breathe,
Just one more time is all I need.

As the day fades to dark,
It is hard to leave what is in my heart.
The sun will rise again the next day;
I will be ready to do the same.

Only a Dream

Dancing in the moonlight,
In the shadow beneath the trees,
Kissing as we dance,
It seemed so real to me.

I hesitated to take it in;
It certainly felt real.
The long, tight embrace
I can still almost feel.

Your breath upon my lips,
A sweetness I still taste.
Looking deep into your eyes,
As I touched your face.

Every kiss more tender,
Deeper than the first;
It stirs a fire in me,
A need to quench my thirst.

As the night grew longer,
I desired more of you.
Each kiss, each touch,
Brought me close to the truth.

As dawn awaited,
Like a brewing storm,
My love for you grew,
Like nothing felt before.

I could not hold back,
My passion as it rose.
Unknown heights never felt,
Wanting you more and more.

Now, as I lie awake,
As real as it does seem,
I hesitate to think
That it was but a dream.

Open Door

I did not ask, and he did not tell,
Though it was clear to me.
He holds tight to his feelings,
Rarely letting others see.

He is okay with me sharing,
All my heart's desire.
But he, for whatever reason,
Holds tight to his fires.

I can only guess, it's a matter of trust,
That he had been hurt before.
But I only want to know him,
That and nothing more.

I had hoped by now, to gain his trust.
It is really important to me.
To get to know all of him,
The part he hides so deep.

He pushed me away,
When the pain crept in.
I thought I had lost him for good,
Even as a friend.

Now he has slowly opened the door.
Though I cannot see through his pain.
My only hope for us,
Is that the opened door remains.

When Doors Will Not Open

The door was closed, the window shut.
Both were locked from the inside.
Those trapped within the house,
Were looking for a place to hide.

No one dare to look out.
Though the curtains were drawn.
Outside things were still,
As though nothing was wrong.

Inside, they all were panicked,
Trapped with not escape plan.
Wondering if they might all parish,
At such an evil hand.

No one ventured near the door,
Or look through the window glass.
They only hovered in the corner,
Waiting for something unknown to pass.

There was nothing outside to keep them in.
No one held a secret key.
No one inside the house was wise enough,
To set the others free.

What a Picture Tells Us

A picture is worth a thousand words,
But yet can leave us speechless.
We hold the image in our minds,
Not knowing when it will leave us.

We keep it close to our heart,
Not sharing at any cost.
Thinking that if we share,
The value will be lost.

Some pictures are meant to share,
Others not shared in the least.
Keeping the images close,
For only a few to see.

Intimacy can be a tricking thing,
Pictures, words, and deeds.
Keeping secrets just between two,
Can be a beautiful thing.

The precious moments of the heart,
Much like the blowing wind.
Is the validation we seek,
When secrets are shared by friends.

When Dreams Awake

When I wake at night,
My thoughts are always of us.
What it will feel like,
When I finally feel your touch.

Your lips tightly pressed to mine,
The touch of your hand,
The warmth of your skin,
My heart cannot comprehend.

Our bodies will become one,
Tightly intertwined,
The heat of passion flowing gently,
With no care or thought of time.

What we both thought unlikely,
Now possesses our dreams.
But now it is time and distance,
That is our enemy.

But time is but for a moment,
Never standing still.
It cannot stop our hearts' desire,
Our dreams will be fulfilled.

The distance, too, is temporary,
Like the waves upon the sea.
Each moment that passes,
Brings you closer and closer to me.

The Search

It was barely dark, the night was falling.
The sky was cloudy, the search was calling.
I could no longer see the light.
The stars were hidden from my sight.

There was no moon to be seen.
Darkness covered everything.
A chill filled the air, as it was damp.
I could see nothing with my lamp.

What I search for, it's hard to say.
But I search for it anyway.
Walking in the cold, dark night,
I can only assume, searching for light.

Not to light my way at all,
For I knew the long and short way home.
Apparently, I search for more,
Something I had not felt before.

Though I could not complete my search.
My heart was broken, and hurt.
I still held fast to my hope,
That one day I might come to know.

That what I searched for could be found,
Not in normal places around.
But in my soul, my mind, my heart,
That is where my search must start.

For in ourselves, we hold the key,
To all we seek that makes us free.
Our happiness is not by chance.
We play the music that makes us dance.

Even when the music stops,
We still keep the memories in our heart.
No one can take that from us,
Not even those we choose trust.

So deeper still I must look,
To find the things not read in books,
For we trust our heart, it's who we are,
To help us find the place to start.

If You Aren't Asleep

"I cannot wait for us to be joined."
Words I read once before.
My body longed for his touch.
His kisses and so much more.

My passion was almost too much to bear.
He felt this as well.
He wanted all of me,
The touch, the taste, the smell.

I imagined our first kiss.
His hands upon my face,
His fingers running through my hair,
When finally his lips I taste.

His beard is rough against my skin,
But only excites me more.
I long to be in his arms,
A feeling not felt before

Letting down my guard,
Intertwined in moments heated,
With no one watching,
Keeping all of our secrets,

The idea it's just ours,
Something only for us to share,
Pushes our desires higher,
Something special and rare.

Yet in the moments passing,
Who knows where things will fall.
I am ready for what lies ahead.
I know he wants it all.

Climbing Through the Window

It was late at night, my heart ached,
For his touch and his taste.
My room was dark and somewhat cold.
I long not for sleep but him to hold.
It was quiet, a still night.
There was darkness, absence of light.
Yet with each moment that passed by,
I want him here by my side.
I did not care from which he came,
Only once here, that he remain.
The night grew closer to midnight.
I wanted him to hold me tight.
As I was about to give in,
I thought I saw something dim.
At my window there was a knock,
A gentile wrapping, very soft.
At first all I felt was fear,
Until I could see through the darkness clear,
Climbing though my window, my heart's desire.
He was here to quench my fire.
Quietly, he joined me in bed.
Being careful where he laid his head.
He kissed me gently, long and deep,
Taking my breath away, I could not speak.
As his body pressed to mine,
We both lost care or thought of time.
He made me feel like none before,
Leaving me wanting so much more.

The Heart Matters

Part Two

Being Chased by a Bear

The wind blew from the north.
The trail was rough and cold.
I really hope I survive,
For this story must to be told.

It was late December, a cold winter day,
Most people in their homes,
But I had ventured out it seems,
To take a leisurely stroll.

At first the beauty took me in,
I found hope and solitude here.
But my feeling would not last,
It quickly turned to fear.

I watched as the deer pranced about,
The rabbits in the nearby field,
The trickling stream called to me,
The sights and sounds surreal,

The sun rose over the forest trees.
The dew danced away with time.
I was lost in myself,
Looking for peace inside.

I did not notice the watcher,
So close but yet concealed.
As I recount this tale,
It still feels all so real.

As I continued to self-reflect,
A sound came from behind.
I did not recognize the growling,
But it was a warning sign.

At first I hesitated,
Too afraid to face my fear.
As I cautiously turned,
The sound I heard grew near.

I am not one to make up lies,
Or even tell half-truths.
I am not sure how,
But I am living proof.

The bear straight up charged.
I had no time to think.
The only thing I could do,
In that moment, fight or flee.

I am not much for fighting bears,
Not something I care to do.
I turned and ran toward the stream,
The bear was in pursuit.

Not sure exactly what happened next,
My memory is unclear.
I am only thankful,
That the bear was distracted by the deer.

The distraction gave me ample time,
To hide among the trees.
I waited there for a long long time,
Until dark, I could no longer see.

I careful plotted my course,
Back to my home place.
I survived to tell the story,
Of the bear chase.

Over Before It Starts

I long for his touch, tasting his lips,
Feeling the passion of our first kiss,
Secluded cabin, mountains side,
Wanting more, but trying to hide.

But yet I could not walk away,
He lured me closer day by day.
Now my body aches for his,
Wanting more than that first kiss.

Time can be an evil cast,
Holding secrets from our past,
Not letting us go where we desire,
Keeping us frozen away from the fire.

Our hearts break before we begin,
Forcing us to turn within.
To find the courage to walk away,
When we really just want to stay.

Passion gives into heated desire,
Keeping us close to the fire.
The fire will burn us, we know its true,
I cannot help it, I am drawn to you.

There is little hope that this ends well.
I am setting myself up to fail.
But my heart and body want more it seems,
I am a victim of my dreams.

Dreams come and go like melting snow,
Hope fades as we all know.
My broken heart will someday mend,
As I am learning to love again.

What Aroused You the Most?

What aroused you the most?
Is it simply holding her close?
Is it the taste of her lips?
Or the curves of her hips?
What makes you crazy every time,
She simply passes by?
Can you in a moment remember,
What makes you stop, feel so tender?
Does her smell make you weak,
Making it hard for you to speak?
Does she know the power she holds,
Or is this a secret you have not told?
I know for me, some secrets are good.
They make us hold tight as we should.
Only sharing with a few,
As we hold tightly to what is true.

Cake and Frosting

I have read much of fire and ice,
But little of frosting and cakes.
What makes the heart desire more,
Is really what's at stake.

The taste is what brings us back.
It's a memory very clear.
But honestly it is the smell,
That first brought us here.

To touch is a great sensation,
One left for us to feel.
But the taste and smell,
Is what makes it all so real.

It is hard not to remember,
What is pressed upon the heart.
Time and truth and love,
Can only be the start.

If we start more slowly,
Will it make thing last,
Or will the inevitability,
Make things move fast?

The soul reaches for things,
The heart can't understand.
We are left with false hope,
Looking at empty hands.

Thinking back to the cake,
Tasting frosting oh so sweet,
We are left with our desires,
Some things we would repeat.

Not much one for sweet sweet treats,
Only leaving us as before.
The desire is ours to bare,
Tasting and wanting more.

But for what our true desire,
Is hard for us to say.
Only knowing that we want,
More of it to taste.

If the cake is before us,
Do we dare partake?
Hoping now with all our heart,
That this is no mistake.

Lust and trust go hand in hand,
Hard for us to define,
Hoping that it works out,
And we are satisfied.

Hope gives into love and trust,
Like the ending of a day,
Honestly, keep the cake,
I prefer fruit anyway.

The Drink

Upon my lips pressed tightly,
The taste I desired most.
It was cold crisp and satisfying.
It was all that I had hoped.

Each sip brought more desire,
A coolness to my soul.
The taste quenched my thirst.
It was all in my control.

As the day passed into evening,
Each sip brought more heat.
To fulfil my one desire,
The taste was somewhat sweet.

My tongue ran across the glass,
As it pressed to my lips.
The more I consumed,
The more I could not resist.

It was somewhat satisfying,
Cold and wet and light.
It was a taste I had before,
But I enjoyed it more that night.

Much like a lover's kiss,
A memory I could not shake.
I longed more and more,
For the sweetness of the taste.

But as morning approached,
And reality set in.
I knew that night,
Was something I would taste again.

A Flower

If our love was a flower,
How would it grow?
Would it be protected?
Or left out in the cold?
Would you water her daily,
Giving her enough sun?
Or would you hope for the best,
Leaving things undone?
Would you tend the earth,
That surround her preciously,
Keeping others away from her,
Protecting all her leaves?
When she finally blooms,
Bringing joy for all to see,
Would you still care for her,
Or simply let her be?
Would her beauty scare you,
Not protected from the sun?
Would you walk away slowly,
Thinking you were done?
Would you let it all end,
Cautiously from the start.
Hoping for the best,
Not wanting to be apart?
If the time came,
For you to part ways,
Would you still love the flower,
Though you could not stay?

Names

For what is in a name?
We all have at least one.
Some we were given at birth.
Other names we earned.

Matters not our name so much,
But our intent from deep inside,
Holding true to ourselves,
Knowing our what, when, and why.

Games are often played,
With a winner insight.
Other games are played,
Just to know who is right.

Names are still there,
What we call someone.
For all the world to know,
Is as important as it comes.

So when giving a name to someone,
We must carefully assess.
Spending lots of time,
To name what is best.

Composting

In piles of leaves and dirt and grass,
All our leftovers we do cast.
Throwing away the unwanted parts,
In hopes of making a new start.

It's not just anything we discard,
We must be careful with our charge.
Leaving only what is best,
Not throwing in the rotting flesh.

Watering much like a plant in spring,
Hoping for the best of things.
With the soil we place upon the heep,
The more benefits we reap.

Only keeping it hidden away,
From others who pass this way.
Some may not understand the need,
For all the work that we heed.

New springs forth from the old,
Life itself will somehow grow.
We may only see with time,
All the things that are refined.

At some point our pile will be,
More than just discarded debris.
It in fact may help us know,
The beauty and power that makes things grow.

The Fire

What fuels a fire, options are many?
It depends on the purpose and intent.
Some fires will destroy all around.
From others warmth is sent.

I don't know much about building fires,
Only what I have witnessed or heard.
But I understand enough to know,
What happens when a fire is stirred.

It's not the intent or even the warmth,
That caused the flames to rise.
It sometimes what has started,
That is found deep inside.

Deep inside beneath the rubble,
You will find what caused it to breathe.
But yet as fateful as a lover,
Other things are key.

Rain much like tears,
May cause the fire to die.
Leaving only a smoke-filled trail,
Where hope no longer lies.

Still beneath the pile,
There is what started it all.
At some point or time,
There may be another call.

Chance is a fickle lover,
Kissing and telling no one.
What stirs a fire at sunset,
Can rarely be undone.

If the fire waits till dawn,
There is yet another chance.
Hope can contain the blaze,
Waiting for shadows to dance.

Giving into sunrise,
Fear into hope,
What fuels the deadly flames,
Is not understood by most.

Much like a lover's first kiss,
No one can really know,
What circumstances must exist,
To make the fire grow.

Untying a Knot

Both practical and impractical,
Neither hot nor cold,
Not the beginning or the end
Of a story yet untold.

Daylight and darkness,
Passing without time,
An enigma at the very best,
An empty glass of wine.

Tears brought from laughter,
Heat from a blazing fire,
A rainbow without sunlight,
Giving in to desire.

Hope not yet hopeless,
In a distance yet unseen,
The last flicker of the flame
Of a treasured memory.

Water all around,
But not a drop to drink,
A candle burning dimly,
As the fire grows weak.

Passing through the shadows,
Dancing in the dark,
Brings fleeting joy
To a broken heart.

Confused but yet confident,
That the light may again shine,
And the emptiness we feel
Will not be the glass of wine.

But still we hesitate
To walk hand in hand,
Not knowing full well,
Or beginning to understand.

Life is full of contradictions,
Both hidden and in the clear.
We walk toward the sun,
Despite all we fear.

A Book Unfinished

The cover was hard, but neatly wrapped,
Secure with in its sleeve.
The binding yet unbroken,
Waiting for someone to read.

The pages stiffen slightly,
Crisp as the morning air.
But yet untouched by a hand,
On the desk waiting there.

The title is irrelevant,
Unimportant to say the least.
What is noteworthy at best,
Is what we have yet to read.

Some may start more slowly,
Or finish within a day.
Others may not start at all,
Choosing to walk away.

Those who start the journey,
Though the path may be slow.
May find out things about themselves,
They did not want to know.

Deep inside us all,
If the truth be told,
We hid secrets from ourselves,
We choose not to know.

When we are deeply immersed,
In the pages yet untouched,
Do we look inward,
Our feelings, do we trust?

Some may choose to go the distance,
Revering every page.
Others may find the burden to great,
Simply choosing to walk away.

Just know this is a fact.
If you walk away,
The ending of each chapter,
Still remains the same.

The treasures are not hidden,
From anyone's sight.
By choosing not to finish,
You are surrendering the fight.

The story does not change.
We know this to be true.
Like the sun setting at dusk,
The words will change you.

The Heart Breaks

Pleasure or Pain

Much has been written about pleasure and pain,
Though with a closer look they are really the same,
Each has an emotional tie.
Each can be sparked by a lie.
Hope can be a dance partner, this we are told,
Or somewhere in the middle for none to hold.
Without the taste of sweet wine,
Only, we the bitter find.
Shall we only dance when the music sings,
Waiting for what the song might bring?
Wounded hearts will one day heal,
Allowing both joy and pain to feel.
But as the door sometimes closes,
We pay the price for things not chosen.
The kiss we dared not to take.
The dance we could not risk to make.
The longing for our lovers' touch,
Leaving us only wanting much.
More than my heart can bear,
I only wish that he was here.
Here to feel my gentle kiss,
To no more moments, we will miss,
To dance when the music does not play,
To know a love so deep, its pain,
The pleasure so intensive to feel,
That it could not possible be real.
Yet love, hope, pleasure, and pain,
Leads us to places we don't abstain.
Only now when things are right,
He will be here to hold me tight.
The pain our love may cause, I chance,
For the pleasure will surpass the dance.

Smoke and Mirrors

Through the looking glass we see,
So many possibilities.
We are often guided by our heart,
Sometimes not knowing where to start.

Things are not often as they seem,
Leading us holding on to dreams.
Looking past the daily gride,
Wishing for better times,

Illusions often lead the way,
Fooling others as we stray.
Away from paths we strive to walk,
Misleading so many in our talks.

Smoke can often cloud our views,
Despite our intentions, it's true.
We sometimes walk instead of run,
Afraid of things we have left undone.

Appearances can often deceive,
Leaving us lost with in our beliefs.
Searching for a path hidden,
Hoping that we will be forgiven.

Smoke, like shadows, dances on glass,
Hoping for a moment to pass.
Mirrors often reflect the light,
But only when the angle's right.

Scars Upon His Heart

He would not open up to me.
I scarcely could understand why.
His need for deep deep privacy.
Perhaps he was hiding lies.

Needless to say, my patience grew weary.
I long to know more and more.
I hesitated to push too much.
Afraid he would close the door.

My heart had already decided,
What my mind could not comprehend.
For the heart wants what the heart want,
Until the bitter end.

A tender kiss upon my lips,
A tightly intertwined embrace,
Left me longing more and more,
For he makes my heart race.

Meeting face to face,
What once terrified me to my core,
One day will revile the truth,
Leading to all I have hoped for.

But it is not just mine to consider,
There are scars upon his heart,
That make him tread more cautiously,
And afraid for us to start,

If with patience I must wait,
It will happen in due time.
My heart perhaps will break,
Or his heart will become mine.

To Make Me Laugh

A kiss upon my check,
Is both tender and sweet,
A simple hello can be a sign,
Or even a good-bye,
It is something wonderful from the start,
And make us happy as we part,
A kiss upon the lips,
Is like the wine we sip,
More than a kiss, a touch,
More like a gentle brush,
This kiss leads to the heart,
Sometimes it's a start,
A kiss upon the neck,
Sensuous and clear,
Takes the breath away, removing all our fear,
Either way it tells of passion, desire,
Can lead to hope and the start of a fire,
A single kiss will not do,
It cannot make me fall for you,
You can rest assure,
As I speak only on my behalf,
The quickest way to my heart,
Is to make me laugh.

Barefoot in Winter

When there is snow upon the ground,
Days are dark and cold.
The heart is hanging on,
Still searching for lost hope.

Snow is cold to the touch,
But melts with the morning sun.
Giving promises for the day,
There are better things to come.

With the sun kissing the ground,
The days seem less grim.
The water dances in the light,
Making us whole again.

But in a few short hours,
Darkness will overtake.
Making us less joyful,
Giving in to our mistakes.

Sometimes mistakes guide us,
Leading us to understand.
The depths of our decisions,
The consequences that are at hand.

Lessons learned or victimized,
Each a choice we must embrace.
We can blame others or circumstances,
And sometimes even fate.

Each man walks his own path,
Let us not be confused.
We all make the choice,
On whether to wear shoes.

Shoes make a difference,
It is a choice we must make.
To walking barefoot in the snow,
Is a risk some will take.

Can I Trust You?

The agenda of the heart can speak,
Louder than most can see,
It matters not how we try to protect,
It can sometime lead to regret.

Hope is bedded in our soul,
Not knowing when truths are told.
We protect it the best we can,
Even when we don't understand.

Love is often mistaken for lust,
The fire sparked with just a touch,
Can sometimes lead to even more,
Feeling much deeper than before.

When confronting our feelings,
The conclusions can be misleading.
A kiss, a touch, a taste,
We are often unwilling to face.

But time may heal wounds,
Leaving us too soon.
We did not know why they exist,
Wondering about all the risk.

Deeper than our soul can feel,
More than a broken heart to heal,
The thing that troubled me from the start,
I wonder if you are pure of heart?

I feel you know my heart is pure,
I trust you to keep it safe, secure.
My hope is that above all else,
You will realize what I have felt.

When strangers meet in the dark,
There is rarely enough time to start,
Hoping that we will feel what's true,
My question is: can I trust you?

Trust you not with just my heart,
That is only for the start.
I need to know if you can,
Be trusted to hold my hand?

Keep me warm when I am cold,
Keep the secrets I have told,
Can you hold me extra tight,
And love all of me through the night?

Will it be too much to bear?
Will you always want me there,
Next to you in all your days,
Despite my flaws, love anyway?

Can I trust you, like no other,
When distance between us grows further?
Will you look when I am lost,
Protecting me at all cost?

If I walk away from you,
Will you know my love is true?
I have trusted you from the start.
I hope you don't break my heart.

Sand

There are millions of grains of sand,
Lying in the desert and by the sea.
Some will be washed away,
Others may be used for things.

A sandcastle built by a child,
On a bright summer day,
Will bring joy for a moment,
Until the tide takes it away.

The sea recycles the specks,
That lie upon its shore.
Not leaving it the same,
Changing it forever more.

It is somewhat inevitable,
The changes that life brings,
From the sand upon the shore,
To almost everything.

The sand does not breathe,
It does not have life at all,
But it still obeys the wind,
And all of nature's call.

So in our hand we hold it,
As carefully as we can,
Knowing if we grip too tight,
It will slip through our hand.

If we hold to loosely,
The wind blows it away,
But the truth of the matter,
It was never meant to stay.

Like the castle on the beach,
On a bright summer day,
We can enjoy it for a moment,
Until it is washed away.

Broken Glass

When glass breaks, it sounds an alarm.
A warning of danger, there could be harm.
The shattering is all so real,
It freezes us for a moment, standing still.
Sometimes we can put together the pieces,
Like sorting a puzzle with no reason.
With glue and patients, we have a chance,
To make what was, whole again.
But what if the broken glass,
Is something deep from our past,
We no longer care to mend,
Or even consider it whole again.
Will we toss it in the trash,
Forgetting that it was broken glass?
Or careless, with no intent,
Let it cut us deep within.
Will we leave it like all the rest?
Hoping someone will clean the mess.
Broken glass upon the floor,
May make it harder than before,
To walk away or maybe run,
Before we see the setting sun,
Can it be the glass itself,
Was really meant for someone else?
Should we just let it be,
Looking now for better things?
Carefully, we make a choice,
To walk away with no voice.
To dance around the brokenness,
Despite our desires for a kiss.
The kiss is my lips on the glass,
That was hastily pushed to the past.
Broken into pieces, like my heart,
The glass was whole at the start.

Like so much life has dealt,
The deep cut is what I felt.
To make the glass unbroken still,
Is to know that love is real.

When the Cold Wind Blows

When the nights have been too long,
And the days dark and cold,
The harsh north wind plays a song,
Of a story not yet told.

My heart needs the warmth,
I can find only in your arms.
I wish I had been less foolish,
And given into your charms.

I long to know your touch,
And the tenderness of your kiss,
Feeling your body against me,
This is all I hope and wish.

I feel you're fading away,
Maybe, for distance and time,
Holding on to something,
That was never even mine.

Maybe it's the wind,
That has swept your heart away.
I wish I had the courage,
To with patience, wait.

I feel no matter what I do,
There is for us no chance.
My hesitation cost us this,
There will be no song to dance.

My Happy Place

Anticipations, excitement, and cheer,
Are emotions that bought me here.
The water is deep but warm,
Heated by the rising sun.

I hesitate to take a chance.
The water is clear at first glance.
Into the water I cautiously step,
Thinking now with some regret.

What will happen in this passing day?
Will I be able to enjoy my play?
Will it all be as I have thought?
Or will it be so hard fought?

At an early age, I learned to walk.
Not long after I began to talk.
Somethings came easier it seems.
Some were harder than other things.

But for the water, I have no fear.
Pool, lake, or ocean, clear,
It is the happiest place of all.
I often hear her beckon call.

The taste of salt upon my face,
Takes me back to another place.
A place where time stood still.
A place where I go to heal.

But with the sand between my toes,
There is always hope to know.
I have memories deeply saved,
That cannot be washed away by waves.

The Heart Shatters

Precipitation

When water falls from the sky,
It comes in all different kinds,
Lightly misting, to heavy down pours,
To frozen stuff that can block our doors.

What makes it such a wondrous thing,
Is that sometimes in the midst of spring,
It brings with it wind, a gusty gale,
With storms that can produce hail.

Hail is not the frozen stuff of dream.
It is harmful and often breaks things.
Leaving a destruction field, a path,
With clean ups required in the aftermath.

The smell of the air when the rain has cleared,
Make my heart soar with no fear,
Reaching the pentacle of delight,
The sound of rain deep into the night.

The sound stirs me deeper still,
Like longing for a lover's feel.
In a sweet heartfelt embrace,
Desiring more of him to taste.

Within the storm, snuggled deep,
Laying in his arms, secrets to keep,
Press tight and closer still,
His body against mine, with all to feel.

Desire rising as the moments pass,
Hoping that it all will last.
At least long enough before we part,
To know the love that is in our hearts.

Enduring Winter

When I walked outside today,
It was so cold, I did not know
I would find myself out there this long.
Wanting to be inside where its warm,
No one made me go outside.
At this moment, I don't even know,
Why I ventured out at all.
It is so cold, dark, and damp.
Who would find joy out here?
I suppose there are those who
Might find it refreshing and clean.
But I am not that person at all.
I do not like winter, cold, or snow.
No one can convince me otherwise.
I know that I am right, you see.
I love the warmth, light, and sun,
When days are longer not dark at all,
When birds sing and shadows dance.
Because the sun is bright in the sky.
The world is filled with hope and joy.
It is the best time of the year.
I will endure the winter cold,
For doing so helps me appreciate,
When it is time for spring.

One Dozen Tears

One dozen tears I shed for you,
Not one less or even more.
I had long so deeply for your touch.
I was taken in by your allure.

I had hoped you were the one.
I would no longer have to search.
But time was not my friend at all,
It may well end in hurt.

You made me feel as no one had.
Maybe that was just your play,
But now I see more clearly,
This was just your game.

I wondered why you targeted me,
With so many other to choose.
They would play the games,
You wanted to play. This leaves me confused.

I believe that you care,
As much as you can.
But for me I need so much more,
Not sure you can understand.

I know that you are afraid,
Of loving someone like me.
My passion is so intense,
It makes it hard to breathe.

I wish you would let your guard down.
Let me love you like only I can.
Making you feel what you never felt.
But instead you turned and ran.

The truth of the matter is,
I do not know what to do.
The heart wants what the heart wants,
In this case that is you.

When Darkness Returns

I felt the darkness closing in.
It had been gone so long.
I had hoped I was past this place.
That I had grown more strong.

He showed me the door once locked.
The one I had held on to so tight.
He made me feel whole again,
Giving me the strength to fight.

But in a single moment,
His truths became lies.
The tears I shed now,
For a pain so deep inside.

He could have left it alone,
Not started things at all.
We could have just been friends.
But I guess that is my fault.

I cannot fault him for his actions.
I can feel him hesitate with fear,
We want different things.
This is crystal clear.

Though we may not have met,
That does not change a thing.
My feelings for him are real,
And the hurt still remains.

Distances and a closed door,
Will not change what I have felt.
It is not what I had hoped for,
It is the hand I was dealt.

I Swam On

I swam until my heart no longer hurt.
It was a pain I had never felt before.
Confusion, love, frustration, and hate,
Were all rolled up into one.
It was not the time I had planned,
Or the simple hope for love,
But I was broken from the inside,
So I swam until the hurt was gone.
I swam and swam and swam some more.
I could not make the pain stop.
I was so broken, I could barely breathe,
But I swam on.
One hour turned into two.
Lap after lap I thought of him.
More and more I felt the pain.
It would not stop.
So I swam on.
I felt that he had betrayed me,
But that really was not the case.
I was mad at myself for the chance I did not take.
So I swam some more.
I swam so I might forget or even ease the pain.
But neither time nor distance made the pain go away.
Finally after four thousand yards, I stopped,
Not because the pain was gone.
I had nothing more to give.
My body was completely drained.
My shoulders ached as did my thighs.
My heart ached just the same.
My mind was somewhat fuzzy,
And feeling a bit waterlogged.
There was water in my left ear.
But the pain in my heart was still strong.
With all my rational thoughts at hand,
I pressed on, with no regret.

Four thousand yards, was just enough,
For me to clear my head.
I knew he was not faithful,
Nor was there a reason for him to be.
We were not yet lovers.
We have not even met face to face.
I was hoping swimming would ease the pain.
Regret is a bitter dance partner,
That time and water can't wash away.
The hours I spent in the pool,
Did make me hopeful.
There is no end to the journey,
Even once it has begun.
It is not the destination,
But the path we take that matters.
Some only long for the path,
Walking closely to the streams.
I long for both path and destination.
My heart cannot take much more.
I can only swim so far.
The hurt that has broken me.
I feel from inside.
Given both chance and wisdom,
Next time I am asked to dance,
I will not wait for the music to play,
Before I begin to sing.

The Pain He Hides

Emotionally, he was not ready,
For what is required to love me.
I feel his heart was heavy,
From things I could not see.

I think that he was searching,
For what I do not know.
But the sad truth of the matter,
Hurts more than I care to show.

He was very well spoken.
His laughter was a delight.
But down deep inside,
I felt demons he had to fight.

The promise of tender kisses,
For all of me to feel.
I know he meant what he spoke,
Even if it was not real.

He may well be living in a fantasy,
Only time will tell.
I do not know my place with him,
It is hidden behind a veil.

Despite this world confusion,
I still long with him to dance.
Holding tight to the possibility,
Somehow there is a chance.

Not for endless love,
Or things of fairy tales,
But a strong bond between us,
That only time can heal.

Healing what was not broke,
But simply protected like glass,
Wondering in all of this,
Can it somehow last.

I don't know his capacity,
To give deeply of himself,
I feel he is hiding secrets,
Putting them high upon a shelf.

Despite what he is guarding,
Protected with a glove,
I am sure of one thing,
Pain can be healed with love.

But love can only be enough,
When he lets others see.
I can only offer him my heart,
I cannot make him take in from me.

But at this pivotal moment,
All I can do is wait.
Hoping he opens up to me,
Before it is too late,

It is not that I will desert him,
My heart is much to kind.
I only know that some heart aches,
Cannot even be healed with time.

I could spend the rest of my life,
Hoping for him to heal.
But I am not sure that's enough,
If he does not let me near,

I doubt he even realizes,
The pain he is holding in.
I will wait with patience,
Being here as a friend.

Lies Not Told

My heart ached not from the lies he told.
He was good at keep them close.
My heart hurt for what he would not say.
It may sound crazy but it hurt just the same.
For what seemed like months,
He flirted relentlessly.
I am not innocent, I participated freely.
But as the time grew near for us to meet,
He pulled away, became more distant.
I can only surmise why.
It is not like he was the faithful kind.
And he told me this much at first.
But I was hoping for love not lust.
Still I am somewhat confused.
I do not know exactly what I should do.
Should I tell him how I feel?
Knowing that would seal the deal?
Forcing him to show his hand.
Might be more than he can stand.
Waiting here, is breaking my heart.
At this point, I don't know where to start.
I feel broken for us both.
This could have been special or I had hoped.

But we all make choice every day.
I guess yours was to walk away.
How can you talk so intensely of love?
Then walk away as if there was none.
I know we will not meet.
That does not make this easier in the least.
I had wanted so much more.
You gave me hope like none before.
So here, I shed my hundredth tear.
Still wishing that you were here,

To kiss me and hold me tight,
To let me know things are alright.
But at this point only you know,
Which of the lies you have told.
What could have changed in a weeks time?
I looked for clues, that I did not find,
But you have made it clear to me,
We have no ties, you are free.
There will be no meeting of our hearts.
Our love will not have a start.
I am more broke now than before.
I wish you had not opened that door.

Your Ugly Scars

When people think they know you,
Sometimes they see who they are,
As a reflection in the mirror,
Without your ugly scars,

But if they really know you,
They see deep into your heart,
They see past all the fences,
And don't mind your ugly scars,

As you look into the mirror,
What do you see this far?
Do you see the pain and suffering,
That caused your ugly scars?

Does his touch excite you?
Do you feel his love start?
Are you afraid of his feelings,
When he sees your ugly scars?

Time may heal some wounds,
Even those upon our heart.
But ever healed wounds,
Can leave ugly scars.

Do you seek isolation,
As if a distance star?
Pushing everyone away,
Not showing your ugly scars.

When tears have been too many,
And the pain will not part,
Do you hide behind your fear,
And all your ugly scars?

Not What You Expected

I walked away proud and brave,
And live to tale my tale again.
It wasn't what I had hoped for,
But it was the hand I was dealt.

I felt a little less than closure,
Because I did not close the door.
But I took back my heart,
Safely away it is stored.

You lured me with passion promised,
And I fail like you knew I would.
I can't say I tried to resist,
Even if I could.

I hold no grudge or resentment.
It is just the way things are.
Some of us feel more deeply,
When it comes to matters of the heart.

I am not saying you don't have feeling,
But maybe I am, just the same.
I was the one left standing,
Alone in the cold cold rain.

With out an ounce of shelter,
To protect me from the cold.
You tried to take it all from me,
Down deep to my very soul.

But I am not the least bit bitter,
For I have grown more strong.
I know that one day you will come for me,
I am sure, I am not wrong.

It remains to be seen, how you play your hand.
Though this is not a game.
I wonder how you will feel,
To see how much I have changed.

You had your shot, when I was weak.
You could have had me all.
But you were way too busy,
Answering another's call!

We all pay the price for our choices.
I have escaped my heart in tacked.
I can't say it wasn't painful,
Let's face it, facts are facts.

So I live to love another day.
Who knows, you, it might be.
But only if you are truly ready,
To give all of yourself to me.

If I Were a Flower

I can only imagine and feel things in my heart,
Hope, love, frustration are a few to start.
But each of these emotions can cause us pain,
Wrapped up in a blanket with little left to gain.

Walking along a path, that we were meant to run,
Not really understanding why things became undone.
The grass might be greener, on the other side of the fence,
Do we dare cross over to try to begin again?

We see the trees tall and lean, dancing in the breeze.
We feel the wind against our face, putting us at ease.
Long ago, when time stood still, we each had a desire.
But much like others, we dance too close to the fire.

We did not burn our clothing, but smoke began to rise.
Reminding us of the importance of keeping things in sight.
Focused on the path ahead, not looking in the past,
Makes it really difficult, to answer questions asked.

All streams lead to bigger water, a path for each to take.
It doesn't happen overnight, it is no mistake.
The water is important, the very breath of life.
So precious is this substance, we will search into the night.

Water is the catalyst that makes everything grow.
It comes in many forms, rain, sleet and snow.
But if I were a flower, planted safely and concealed,
Would there come a time when I would be revealed?

If I were a flower, would I be loved and kept safe?
Would you protect me or just give me away?
Would my beauty be enough, to draw you near?
Or would you try to hide me not out of love but fear?

If you do not desire my beauty or want my love,
Would you keep me from other, protect with a glove?
When my season of my beauty has faded into dusk,
Would you love me still, being someone I can trust?

If you would not still love me, then simply walk away.
You know, both of us will be hurt if you decide to stay.
There will be no hard feelings not on my behalf,
Because if I were a flower, these feelings I do not have.

Best Night Sleep

I slept the best I had in weeks,
Because I did not wait on him.
My honesty had set me free.
My heart now belonged to me again.

It's not that I wanted this to happen.
But I felt he gave me little choice.
He was clearly losing interest.
Oh well, that is his lose.

He had opened a door, once closed,
I held tight but not yet locked.
I kicked it in myself, you see,
With the key and secrets I held.

I know he does not understand me,
Maybe he does not even care.
But the power that I have gained,
Helped me grow beyond myself.

Seeing things as they have always been,
Made it much easier to sleep.
I will rest much easier at night,
Knowing I am true to myself.

Hope for a
New Beginning

When Hope Returns

I heard the popping of the can,
As the tab was quickly pulled.
The drink was cold, wet, and crisp,
Like most drinks, and obviously full.
But the weather was also cold,
Cold, wet, and dark.
It reminded me of how I felt,
Sometimes things just are.
It isn't that I longed for him,
Oh I am such a liar.
I long for so much more.
I could not control my desire.
I wanted him to kiss me,
Long and deep and hard.
I had even dreamed about him.
My body for him starved.
His touch must be so special,
Like nothing I have ever felt.
I wanted him close to me.
I wanted nothing else.
I do not know if this dream,
Will pass beyond this stage.
Honestly it is not fair,
To keep my heart caged.
My passion runs so deep,
Deeper than the river runs.
I am somewhat optimistic,
But still sticking to my guns.
My love will not be on his terms,
Though I want him to stay.
I must hold tightly to myself,
And not give myself away.

A Foggy Sunrise

I slept deep and sound.
Nothing disturbed my slumber.
I arose to no alarms.
Nothing really woke me.
I shuffled to the kitchen.
Where coffee was to brew.
I had prepared it the night before.
It is just easier that way.
I flip the switch on the maker.
I could smell the aroma rise,
And hear the water trickling.
I wander through the house,
Waiting for my morning to start.
I hesitated for a moment,
Contemplating my next course.
Should I shower first,
While the coffee brews,
Or step outside and watch the sun rise?
I waited for the coffee.
With the cup in one hand,
My phone in the other, I took a little stroll.
Stepping into the mist,
Looking across the mountains,
It was a foggy sunrise.
I captured the moment.

Counting Snowflakes

When the winter days have been too long,
For the south that could be a week.
Looking across the frozen lawn,
Ice crystals kissing each blade of grass,
I ask myself just today,
What does any of this mean?
In a moment that has already passed,
On the coldest day of the year,
I do not dare to tread where ice abounds.
I am careful where I place each step.
The wind is cold and takes my breath.
Longing now for warmer days,
Which will not come soon enough,
Cold weather is only good for cuddling.
Wrapped in a blanket in front of a fire,
Snuggling deep in a lover's embrace.
If only he was here now,
Not far away in another place.
I could be counting the days and hours,
Until we are at last joined.
But instead, I am counting snowflakes.

The Moment That Changed My Destiny

What I could only give of myself,
It was not his to take,
My heart, my mind, my soul,
Only I could give away.

He was somewhat charming.
I was fearful for my heart.
I should have tread more cautiously.
I knew that from the start.

He had a deep drive and passion.
That drew me to his flame.
I know now despite it all,
I will never be the same.

I long not just to know him,
But I desire it all.
The touch, the smell, the taste,
All of nature's call,

I feel it is more than passion,
That I seek to find in him.
There is something uniquely special,
That he hides deep within.

Though he tries to hide it.
I can see it in his eyes.
The things he holds deeply.
Many others might despise.

Truth is a rare commodity.
Unfortunately things change.
But I guess it is inevitable.
Nothing can remain the same.

When I think back in years to come,
A single moment will remain.
The moment he entered my life,
My destiny was changed.

When Winter Finally Ends

Winter has been too long.
Spring could still be months away,
I am cold, alone, and nervous,
About what the coming weeks might bring.

For five weeks now, we have flirted,
Shared a laugh and more.
I have shed one thousand tears,
For someone I have never met before.

There is a hopeful promise,
That ours will be a story to tell.
Do things really work out like that?
Perhaps, if so, it is very rare.

If I were into making lists,
Like many of my friends have done,
I could check off every box for him,
Every single last one.

I have tried to hold it close within.
Play things casually.
But sometimes it just hurts so deep,
When I think of what could be.

He has made it somewhat clear.
Though he has given me mixed vibes.
Either he is good at hiding himself,
Or good at telling lies.

I don't even know if time will tell,
Patients is not my game.
I am holding tight to hope,
Maybe he feels the same.

If we are searching for different futures,
I am happy with the hand I was dealt.
I know one day I will look into his eyes,
And see all that he has felt.

The longing for his kiss to taste,
His breath upon my lips,
I cannot think of anything else,
My heart breaking, I would risk.

Chances are it will end.
Badly, no one can really know.
I only know I must take the chance,
Before I let him go.

If it does end badly,
I hope he knows within.
There will never be hard feels,
We will always be friends.

Awake in the Early Morning

When I wake in early morning,
And sleep evades me still.
I often think of you,
Wishing you were here.

Wishing for your tender kiss,
Our lips pressed tight.
Our tongues dancing merrily,
In anticipation of the delight.

Our bodies are intertwined,
With skin upon skin, heat.
With a greater longing,
For both of us to meet.

Pushing through the passion,
And our physical desire.
In each other's arms,
We find what quenches our fire.

There is a sweet sweet dampness,
For each of us to taste,
Longing more and more,
Neither of one of us hesitate.

Our desire grows much stronger,
Even out of our control.
We lay together for endless hour,
Each other do we hold.

Sometimes the Weatherman is Wrong

The weatherman says we should expect snow.
For you freaks, I hope you are happy.
Snow could be my least favorite thing,
Next to cooking and cleaning and paying taxes.
I can think of a few times when snow might be grand.
If you were here, and we were alone.
Then perhaps, I might welcome the snow.
But you are not here and I will not be alone.
So here I am, with the prospect of snow.
The temperature has already dropped from 56 to 35,
And getting colder with each moment that passes.
I could be angry with you, no one to keep me warm.
But since we have not met, I will let that pass, for now.
Somehow in all the confusion and time.
Who knows where it goes, or why it passes fast or slow.
I still hold fast to the hope that we will one day be together.
I know many might think I am foolish.
But after all, what is hope for? except to fill us with anticipation.
About things we have never felt before, good or bad.
I have a keen imagination, so I have been told.
Not sure it was a compliment, now that I think about it.
But that is what dreams are made of.
If the moment never comes, when we shall meet.
I will press on with all my heart, for the moments,
In my heart and soul when we were together in spirit.
I felt you as much as I have felt anyone, ever.
Others may not understand, the spirit that drives desire.
But even if we never meet, my time has been well spent,
Not chasing dragons or ghost or even butterflies.
My heart has been searching for a long time.
Knocking at a door that would not open.
I only needed someone to show me the key.
The key that I held in my hand, my tightly closed hand.
Once opened, I was free to unlock the door to my heart,
And look for love again.

He Took My Breath Away

He kissed my lips, my breathing stopped.
I felt a rush through my body.
It was cold outside but I felt very very hot.
One hand upon my face, the other in my hair.
His tongue dance in my mouth, I lost all care.
He moved slowly but with intention.
Each touch strategically placed,
From my face to my neck to my waist.
His mouth soon followed, each kiss tender still,
The taste, the smell, the touch, all of him to feel.
I could barely contain my excitement.
He pulled me tight against him.
I felt his excitement too.
As he pressed hard against my body,
I knew!
The moments of long waiting,
The hours of wondering if,
In that single moment, I felt it all from that first kiss,
I am unsure of the timing, whether right or wrong.
I cannot recall the music, but I do remember the song.
With no hesitation,
He kissed me deeply more and more.
His skin was warm against mine.
A feeling I had long imagined.
But my imagination cannot compare,
To the pleasure I was feeling.
There are no words to describe.
With each touch my passion rose.
I never knew I could reach such heights.
His skills were undeniable with tenderness and care.
He made sure that my desires were met.
More tenderly each time, he kissed me gently.
His lips pressed to mine.
He took my breath away.

Making Sense of It All

Leaping Off a Cliff

I could not breathe, my chest felt tight.
I waited impatiently through the night.
To hear the words once spoken clear.
"I want all of you, I wish you were here"
My imaginations ran wild, more active than a child.
Had he grown bored with me? Did he no longer want to meet?
My heart did not hurt yet, I was thankful, with no regret.
For all the passion he had unlocked,
I did not want it to stop.
Now there is no reason, we have passed beyond that season.
I have trusted him with my soul, now it is out of my control.
I hesitate with each message sent, I do not know his intent.
I cannot imagine he would go away, I also I don't think he will stay.
Either way the ride has been a thrill.
Even the parts that were not real.
I can only feel in my heart, sitting here looking at the clock.
I know, no mistakes have been made.
Life is just funny that way.
If our paths never cross, I will not count it as a loss
Sometimes we must take risk, like the moment of a first kiss.
When hope seems somewhat clear, there is a total lack of fear.
So when I stand at the edge of that cliff,
I will take a running start and leap off of it!

Stronger Than the Storm

There is an eerie silence no one hears.
The crackling of footsteps upon the ground,
The kissing of the wind at night,
Shadows dancing with no music playing,
Keeping a rhythm all to themselves,
Only some can feel the pain that deep,
A kiss, a touch, a warm embrace,
Leaving us wanting more,
The storm may pass with no damage,
Or leave a pathway of destruction,
Devastated by wind, rain or snow,
Hope lost before the storm,
Storms may not give way to better days,
We can hope, but there is no guarantee,
That anything will be the same,
That is just the way things are,
Far away or even close,
We hold tighter than anyone expects,
Survival is not the goal,
Our strength comes deep from within,
Struggling again to see through the dark,
Our hearts become one, despite it all,
The kiss we dare to take,
Is what makes it all so real,
Feeling deeper within our soul,
A story told from the heart,
Lasting through the darkest night,
We must be stronger than the storm,
Otherwise we will not find love.

In a Forest Green

The forest is lovely this time of year.
There is a quietness and peace within.
A hopeful song I sometimes hear.
I cherish but rarely share with friends.

But I do share with my lover, heart's desire.
For I trust him to keep my sacred truths.
The ones I hold close to the fire.
I have long hoped for since my youth.

Youthful thoughts are often a fool's dream.
Dancing among the shadows in the dark,
Hoping there are no watchers to see,
My lustful dance from my heart,

For deep down in my heart I truly know,
A desire so strong I cannot let it go.

The Darkest Path

When the road has been too dark and cold,
Others have found their way home.
It's not that the road was always dark,
Some of the darkness came from my heart.

Often the heart can light the way,
Given us hope when we go astray.
But lately my heart has had no light,
Making for even darker nights.

I lie alone think of what could be.
I wonder if he is thinking of me.
I once thought I was his one desire.
The one sent to quench his fire.

Now I don't know my purpose here.
It is quite cloudy and unclear.
Am I here to light his way?
Even knowing I cannot stay.

I cannot travel where he must go.
The path is treacherous and unknown.
I tied my heart to his before,
I knew the path he was searching for.

Now I must face what the future brings,
Still unclear about so many things.
Will my love be enough to guide his soul?
Helping him face the bitter cold.

Should I walk away now while I can?
Knowing in his heart he will understand,
My heart to him will always belong,
No matter the lyrics of his song.

Because of the Choices Made

I don't know where this road might lead.
It may wind endlessly back upon itself.
It could lead to a cliff so high,
That I will be able to touch the sky.
Or maybe into the deep dark woods,
Where secrets hide and lies are told.
Along the way,
Some will be touched,
Some will be hurt,
Some will be loved,
All will be changed not because of the path,
But because of the choices made.

Time itself does not stand still.
Games are sometimes both won and lost,
Before the first whistle blows.
Leaving us all to doubt the validity of the game.
Though some will win, while others lose,
Not because of the game,
But because of the choices made.

But life is not a game.
We all must choose our path with care.
Not knowing if it will lead us where we want to go.
Standing still is not an option.
For soon the cold will come and freeze us where we stand.
Spring will not thaw away the pain.
The bright sun of summer gives us hope,
Making us look for paths not yet known.
Summer may end with unfulfilled promises.
Not because of the long hot days,
But because of the choices made.

Ankle Deep in the Snow

Standing ankle deep in the snow,
Waiting for things to change,
Watching as the snowflakes fall,
Upon the ground and the road.
Others may drive by too fast.
I guess they have places to be.
As for me, I am here for now.
Not knowing how, time will change things.
But still the snow falls.
I wish it was spring or summer.
Hot is so much better than cold.
I know others may not agree.
But they are wrong.
Nothing grows in the cold,
Not love, or lust or even hope.
What could any of this mean?
I barely can comprehend my own feelings.
I feel cold, alone, and afraid in the dark.
My heart does not hurt, but is numb.
Only now in the distance, do I hear sounds,
Not sounds of hope, really,
But sounds of life passing by,
Life continuing despite lost hope.
We may search for days on end,
Or leave things as they were found.
Only time can heal some wounds.
But even then, there will be scars.
A kiss is but a moment taste upon the lips.
It can mean nothing or everything.
I cannot wait to taste that kiss.
And finally learn what it means.
Will it be the beginning of a road once searched?
Or will it be a cliff for me to leap off?
Not knowing if I will land or just keep falling,
With no end or hope insight?

So much to place on a single kiss.
For me I hope it takes my breath away,
Like no other kiss before.
Knowing that it could be my last first kiss,
Makes my heart race.
Still I wonder what it will be like?
When I am no longer ankle deep in the snow,
But intertwined in his arms,
Experience that first of many kisses.

Only Time Will Tell

The rain has been falling for what seems like days,
With no end in sight,
Except for a brief window of time.
Time itself is an interesting concept,
Never standing still or waiting on anyone.
We all want time on our terms.
But that is ridiculous.
Time is what time is,
A measure of existence,
Perhaps!
Or something to be wished away,
In anticipations of things to come or the things that might be,
We invent all different ways to measure.
Why?
Somehow knowing does not change things.
We try to find ways to occupy ours,
Like holding tighter to sand will keep it safe somehow.
Waiting is probably the worst part.
The closer the time gets the harder the wait.
Waiting on a package or an appointment or work to start,
All seem relatively easy.
But when you are waiting in anticipation of love,
That seems like an eternity.
What once was months turned into weeks then days.
So here I sit.
Days away or perhaps still weeks
No one really knows, I sure don't.
I doubt he does.
Some only see what is right in front of them,
Like an opened door or maybe even an unlocked window.
A window for a lover to climb in, in the middle of the night,
To still away what is already his.
But there is still rain and the darkness of night,
With no end in sight, except for the hope of a sun filled day,
That only time will tell.

I Can Only Imagine

I can only imagine what it must be like,
To kiss you and be held tight,
To relax completely in your arms,
Giving in to all your charms.

I can only imagine in the night, dark,
The tenderness of your heart,
When no one else is there to see,
Just how much you excite me.

I can only imagine in the light of day,
How the darkest night will give way,
To pleasure I have not known before,
Leaving me want so much more.

I can only imagine the warmth of your hand,
Touching me like no one else can,
Taking my breath away as only you do,
Falling deeply in love with you.

I can only imagine one kiss will not be enough,
I want all of you, taste, smell and touch,
To know that when I am finally by your side,
All my hopes and fears I no longer hide.

I can only imagine when the time comes for us to part,
I will be leaving you all of my heart,
I have wanted this for so long,
My feelings for you have grown strong.

I can only imagine, with the coming days,
It will be hard to walk away,
I will leave my heart with you,
Hoping that our love is true.

Is Omission a Lie?

Truth and honesty are very important to me.
I try myself not to hide or even deceive.
When does the truth actually become a lie?
Is it when it's withheld or just when it hides?

Is telling only half the truth the same as a fib?
When it is okay to keep things hidden deep within?
Should we always strive to tell all we know?
Even if the truth will destroy someone's hope?

I do not know the answer, though in my heart,
I would hope you trust me enough to be honest from the start.
I know enough and understand trust must be earned,
It is not given freely or something that we learn.

Being pure of heart, not everyone can claim.
It is a rare characteristic, standing close to the flame.
I hope above all else, you know what is true.
I would never do anything intentionally to hurt you.

My hope for me is the same, regardless of how you feel.
You will be honest with me by keeping things real.
Lies only given into more lies and send bridges up in flames,
Leading to endless heart ache with very little to gain.

Why people feel the need to lie or play their little games,
Is very hard to understand, but hurts just the same.
I cannot tell how much faith and trust I have for you.
But somewhere down deep inside, I know you know the truth.

Don't Wait in the Dark

It isn't that I was lost,
As much as I was searching,
Perhaps for the meaning of life,
Or maybe even just meaning.
I look first at the beach.
It was peaceful and calm there,
Maybe too calm.
I needed excitement and love of life
That had been slowly draining from me.
I am not complaining.
My life is wonderful.
But still,
I needed something more,
Something that felt a little more real.
This is a tale that should be told
In many years to come.
Sitting in the darkness, waiting,
Things will not just happen.
So whatever it is you're waiting on,
Go searching in the dark.
Nothing good can come from waiting,
Especially if you wait too long.
Life should be an adventure.
That is the lesson I have learned.
So don't wait for life to happen.
Meet it head on.
What if you slip and fall
On the frozen, icy path?
At least you will have that tale to tell,
More interesting than the last.
Who knows? The path might be clear,
No ice upon the ground.
For whether mountain, sea, or desert,

There is an adventure to be found.
So do not sit in the dark, waiting,
For life will pass you by.
Take a chance, take a step, take a leap
On love, on yourself, on your dreams.
For each moment you spend sitting,
Alone or in a crowded room,
Is a moment lost forever.
It will not return to you.
Don't wait for the next opportunity.
Create it for yourself.
Take that eye-closed leap
Into waters yet unknown.
Fall deeply in love with someone
Forbidden to your heart.
Live as if each day is your last.
Don't care what others think.
Walk as if you have purpose
And somewhere important to be.
Make today that day,
The last time that you waste.
Run instead of walk a path yet unknown.
Go all out for your dreams.
And if you do not have dreams,
Then search until you find
Something deep inside of you,
A passion uniquely yours.
Then throw yourself off the cliff
As if you will sprout wings and fly.

Does Any of this Make Sense?

When time does not stand still,
But yet it does not move forward,
You are stuck.
Not in the mud or in a ditch,
Just stuck.
Unable to move forward,
Impossible to move back,
Even if you could,
The way forward seems scary and unclear,
Like stepping of a dock into muddy water,
Unsure as to how deep it is.
Clear water can be deceiving too,
Crystal clear,
Unable to tell the depth.
What lies below can be more dangerous,
Than what is waiting on the shore,
Beneath it all, there could be nothing,
Nothing but water, mud, silt and fish,
Fish wondering why you are there.
After all, you have invaded their home.
But we, humans rarely see it like that,
The world is our oyster.
I suppose, but oysters belong to the sea.
They have a purpose.
As for me, I am searching for my purpose.
Again,
Hesitating,
Lost,
Wondering,
Does any of this make sense?
In the keenest sense of the word sense
Since when?
Since always?
Since never?

All is lost except for that one ray of sunshine,
The one moment of light that kisses the dew away in the morning,
Giving me all I need to move forward.

Why It Matters

If Walls Could Talk

If walls could talk what would they say,
About all the games that we play.
Would they laugh and make fun of us,
As we give into empty lust?

Would our fantasies be revealed,
Along with secret plots to kill?
Is big brother watching now,
To learn where our truths are found?

What of our password and security codes,
Would they be shared to those unknown?
Would we dare to speak from the heart,
Not knowing where the truth might start?

In our silence, do they know,
What we feel but do not show?
Is it safe for us to trust, share, and love,
Without the protection of a glove?

If any of these things were real,
Do we tell what we feel?
Should we run instead of walk,
Escaping from the walls that talk?

Pandora's Box

When mischief is set free,
All the world is turned around.
Looking for the purpose,
Not sure where it will be found.

The good is thrown away.
Cast out like an empty cup,
Into the trash of the world.
Nothing is quite enough.

What is wrong now seems right.
Evil is perceived as good.
The light in the world is gone.
Darkness reigns before the calm.

Trouble has possessed us all.
We walk with our eyes closed.
Afraid we might find the way,
To the story never told.

The story must be told,
For the good of all mankind.
You cannot do evil,
Expecting good to find.

Sometimes we walk alone.
Sometimes we walk too far.
Sometimes we need to remember,
Pandora's box was just a jar.

But not everything escaped the jar.
Which is something worthy of a note.
The one thing man needs most of all,
Trapped in the jar, is humanity's hope.

Rules of Engagement

There are rules, on so many.
That tell us how to act,
That tell us who we are,
And tell us what are facts,

Rules, in theory
Were created to organize.
But in reality, I feel
That many just hide lies.

Whether true or half true,
You can't have it both ways.
It either is or isn't,
You can't both leave and stay,

But what are the lies,
That we believe to be true?
How do these affect us?
Do we search for hidden clues?

It is dangerous for many,
To search in the dark.
For the truth that evades,
Will only break the heart.

When rules become laws,
All are expected to obey.
Even when we know the truth,
Do we hide our face in shame?

The injustice of reality,
Can be found near.
It is as cold as ice,
Even more than crystal clear.

Knowing what's at risk,
Do we dare to take a stand?
Or simply wait silently,
Afraid of what's at hand.

There will come a time,
When a choice we all must make.
Will you stand with the innocent?
Or will you give into hate?

Evil Around Us

Much has been said of loyalty,
To ourselves, others and country,
Being proud of who we are,
Standing for something in our heart,

Walking a chosen path that's free,
To follow it where our dreams may lead,
To dance to the music when it plays,
Free to leave or even stay,

Some value more these rights,
Other are only looking to fight,
Thinking that their rights matter more,
They are even keeping score,

In the grand scheme of things,
What does a victory really mean,
It does not mean that they are right,
Just because they won the fight,

Truth is found in the heart,
It will tell all who you are,
Evil sometimes will prevail,
Leaving us in a living hell,

We don't lose hope in these times,
Holding fast to the truth we find,
There are others who are willing to fight,
And stand with us for what is right,

When the battle seems all but lost,
Are you willing to pay the cost,
To stand for what is right and true,
To go the distance and see it through,

Those in authority can be wrong,
Causing much pain and needless harm,
Truth is not the same as power,
Some hide behind it like a coward,

Some are willing to just stand by,
Believing all of the awful lies,
Not wanting to get involved,
Not see a problem that can be solved,

At what point does it become too real,
Standing by watching them all kill,
If no one bothers to take a stand,
We all have blood on our hands,

We have a responsibility to other,
To treat them better than our brothers,
Defending them when they cannot,
No matter what the end will cost,

For if we choose to walk away,
Knowing the pain that was caused today,
The privilege and rich will have won,
Paying no price for the things they've done,

Cutting off the head of the snake,
Hopefully will be all it takes,
To rid the world of the pain we feel,
Giving us all time to heal,

But if we don't stand and fight,
To defend others and what is right,
More lives will be lost,
And we cannot afford that cost.

When They Come for You

They came first for the weak and old,
The ones who could not defend themselves.
They labeled them as a threat
And executed them in the street.
Next, they came for the children,
Using them as bait
To lure others out of their homes,
To kidnap, rape, and take away.
Next, they came for those who cared,
Recording the things that were not right
Unlawful, unmoral, cruelty.
They murdered them just the same.
We saw it all, thanks to their bravery.
They label these truth seekers, too,
As a threat to those who reigned.
We watch from the safety of our homes
Or from streets far away,
Trapped in the dilemma between safety and truth.
Many will believe as they are told.
Blind followers are the most dangerous
And the easiest to control.
I pray many will open their eyes,
Seeing for themselves what is true.
Some say we should arm ourselves
To fight and protect what is right.
It seems unclear to me
If this will do good or more harm.
We seem to be at a breaking point,
One of no return.
So this is the question
You must ask yourself
In these dark, dark times:
What will you do in that moment
When they come for you?

The Candle Flame Burns Bright

The candle flame flickered, danced in the shadows.
The night grew darker and cold.
The ice outside had not yet begun to melt.
The wind sang a sad love song, for only a few to hear.
In the distance, there was but silence —
No sounds, no birds to sing.
In the silence of the darkness,
Sometimes hope is lost, or maybe just forgotten.
I relished the times when hope gleamed bright,
Like the brightest stars up in the sky.
But tonight was not that night.
Some will never recover from this moment.
Heartbreak will lead to an unknown place,
Where only darkness lives and no light is allowed.
Others might fight through the webs that led to despair.
Others might just walk away, like nothing happened.
I do not know what path you will choose, nor I for that fact.
I know that in a moment, cold and dark, in an icy field,
Decisions have been made that changed everything,
Maybe forever.
Gone is the innocence when the shadows danced,
And the birds sang with no care.
Now the birds warn us to watch our step out in the icy cold.
But what will we do when the birds no longer sing —
No warning, no calling, no hope, no memory?
Erased from time, as if it never existed.
But we must remember.
We must remember the candle,
And the darkest nights,
When hope was lost but for the candle.
The candle's flame burns brightest in that darkest moment.

This Is Not a Movie

It seemed so surreal, but real it was,
Like something from a very bad movie.
A movie would have had a better script,
With a more predictable ending.
We have no ending in sight,
Only the beginning, few recognized.
The cast would have been vetted,
Many experienced, some new.
And there would have been a plot,
A direction for which the story flowed.
But there was cold and killing and more killing.
Some heroes arose for a moment.
They were shot dead in the streets.
It was cold; the protest grew.
I cannot figure out the plot.
There were men in uniforms and mask.
They seemed quite angry and pushed people,
Innocent people in the cold streets.
I keep watching, waiting for the plot to unfold.
There was tear gas, guns, yelling, killing in the cold.
The snow fell on the bloody streets, white mixed with red.
Some hid, some ran, and the whole nation cried,
Except for some!
We may not have been watching the same movie.
Some rose to take a stand.
Others stood in disbelief.
There were stories on the internet,
Some true, some lies, some created by AI.
But it was cold, and the killing continued in the streets.
It may take years to unpack the plot, the scenes as they are told.
We must all strive always to remember the fallen ones.
For this is not a movie,
It's real, it's dangerous, it's sad, and it may last for years to come.

Special Poems for My Family and Friends

Our Friendships

It was neither here nor there,
Only par for the course.
Some friendships are forged.
Others are a choice.

Ours was a perfect friendship,
Only from time to time.
Though we rarely met in person,
It was mostly online.

Our brief encounters once a year,
Was enough for us to bond.
Over likes, dislike and other things,
Our brain wiring was one.

Though we feel and think,
In many different ways.
There is a level of trust,
With each card we play.

This Year

We made it through our worst year yet.
None of us will ever forget.
It was harder for some than most.
They carried the burden far too close.
No one can judge the price they paid,
To make sure others saw better days.
They picked up the pieces that fail to the ground,
With very little help from those around.
Angels walk among us, they say,
Keeping us grounded, not to stray.
I speak for myself, but others too,
I would not have made it this year without you.

Happy Birthday Julie

Today I miss you more,
Than the day that you left.
You would have been 54,
(Though I think you would prefer
I leave the number out)
I know I am not the only one,
Who feels a pain within.
It is hard to believe,
It's been more than a year.
I would be lying,
If I did not say.
I think about you often,
Almost every day.
You are my family, friend and confidant.
I talk to you and tell you thinks,
That others I cannot.
You are the best keeper of secrets,
Protecting them with your heart.
Talking to you came ease,
That was the best part.
I know others trusted you,
But that was just your style.
I would give almost anything,
To hear your laugh and see your smile.
I am very thankful.
I have memories that last.
You cared so deeply for everyone,
Not judging them for their past.
That is one of the reasons,
You are missed so much.
I know my pain and loss,
Are small compared to some.
Your husband and children,
I can't even image their pain.

You left a legacy of love,
For that we all have gained.
Knowing you has made us better.
You are an example of love.
I know you help protect us,
As you look down from above.

Bickham Script Pro 3 and Cormorant Garamond on LSI Creme
Type and Design by Mackenzie Carey
Cover Design by Cathy Carey

www.ingramcontent.com/pod-product-compliance
Lightning Source LLC
Chambersburg PA
CBHW021827090726
47818CB00077BA/76

* 9 7 8 1 9 7 0 5 3 0 0 2 5 *